T0403009

Look Up!

LEVEL 4

/oi/ear/ /air/

DECODABLES BY jump!

Teaching Tips

Blue Level 4

This book focuses on the phonemes **/oi/ear/air/**.

Before Reading

- Discuss the title. Ask readers what they think the book will be about. Have them briefly explain why.
- Ask readers to point to and say the names of the objects and actions on page 3. On a separate sheet of paper, have them write the words.

Read the Book

- Encourage readers to break down unfamiliar words into units of sound. Then, ask them to string the sounds together to create the words.
- Urge readers to point out when the focused phonics phonemes appear in the text.

After Reading

- Encourage children to reread the book independently or with a friend.
- Ask readers to name other words with /oi/, /ear/, or /air/ phonemes. On a separate sheet of paper, have them write the words.

© 2024 Booklife Publishing
This edition is published by arrangement with Booklife Publishing.

North American adaptations © 2024 Jump!
5357 Penn Avenue South
Minneapolis, MN 55419
www.jumplibrary.com

Decodables by Jump! are published by Jump! Library.
All rights reserved. No part of this book may be reproduced in any form without written permission from the publisher.

Library of Congress Cataloging-in-Publication Data is available at www.loc.gov or upon request from the publisher.

ISBN: 979-8-88524-742-9 (hardcover)
ISBN: 979-8-88524-743-6 (paperback)
ISBN: 979-8-88524-744-3 (ebook)

Photo Credits

Images are courtesy of Shutterstock.com. With thanks to Getty Images, Thinkstock Photo and iStockphoto. Cover - Yaroslav Vitkovskiy, LightField Studio, Bonezboyz. 3 – Africa Studio, Fototocam, Zerbor, Somchai Som.4&5 - xtock, Sergey Mironov. 6&7 - NASA images. 8&9 - Aphelleon, MarcelClemens. 10&11 - Triff, Just Super. 12&13 - Tomsickova Tatyana, Paopano. 14&15 - Orla, Vadim Sadovski.

How many words can you list with  **oi** in them?

Look up at night. How far can you see? Can you see high up in the air?

Can you see the stars? You might see stars on a clear night.

Stars

Stars are big balls of gas that burn. They are boiling hot!

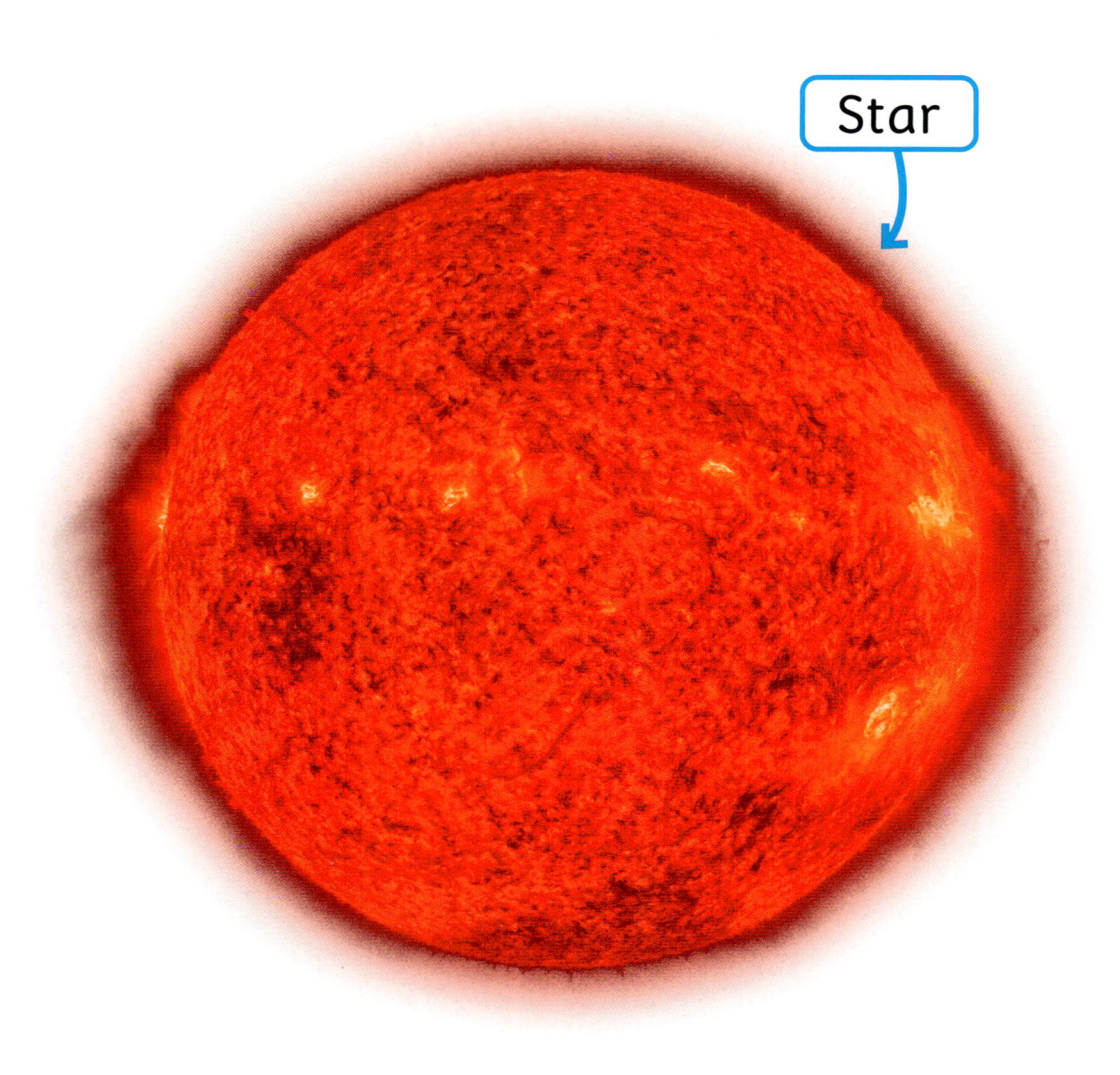

Star

Lots of stars are far from us,
but a big star is near to us.

The Sun is a star. We get light from the Sun. It helps us see.

Part of the planet is light. Part of the planet is dark.

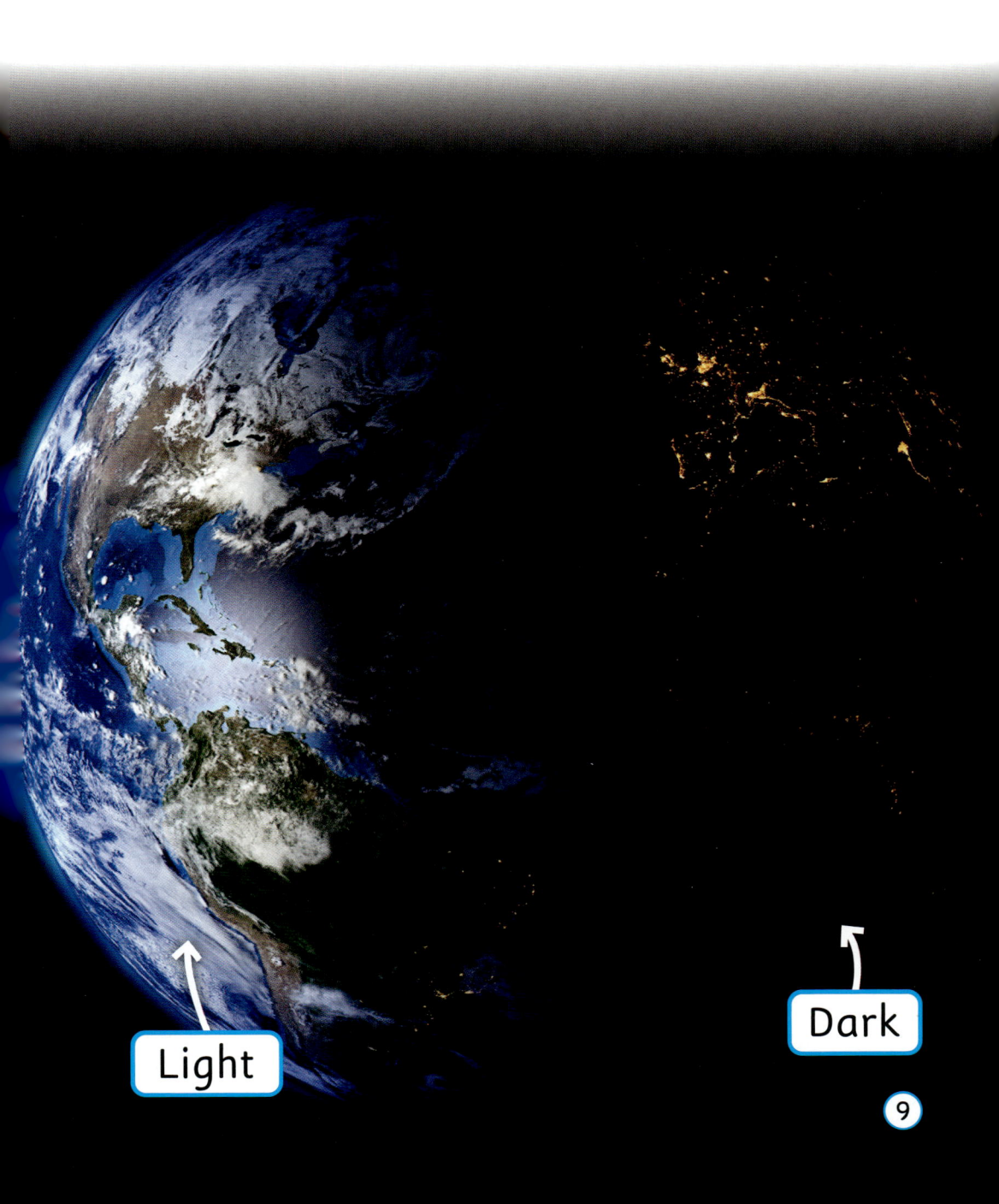

Light

Dark

At night, we do not see the Sun.
We see the Moon.

Can you point to the Moon?

The planet we are on has one moon. The Moon has no air.

I will go to the Moon in my rocket gear! Will you join me? Have no fear!

Saturn is a big planet. It has a lot of rings.

Can you point to the rings?

Mars has a pair of moons. You might see Mars at night as a red dot in the air.

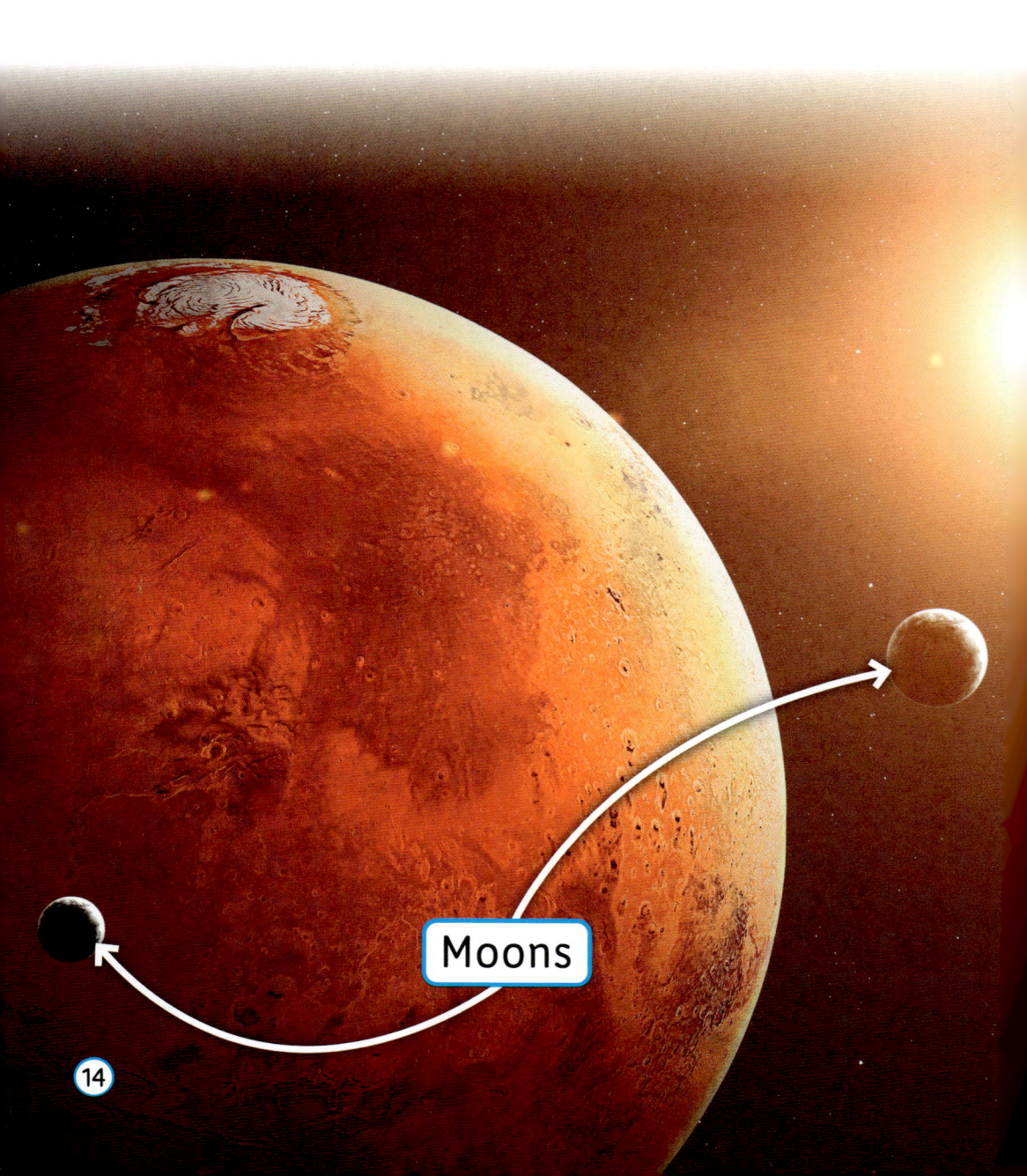

Moons

Mars is not far from us, but we will not go to Mars for years.

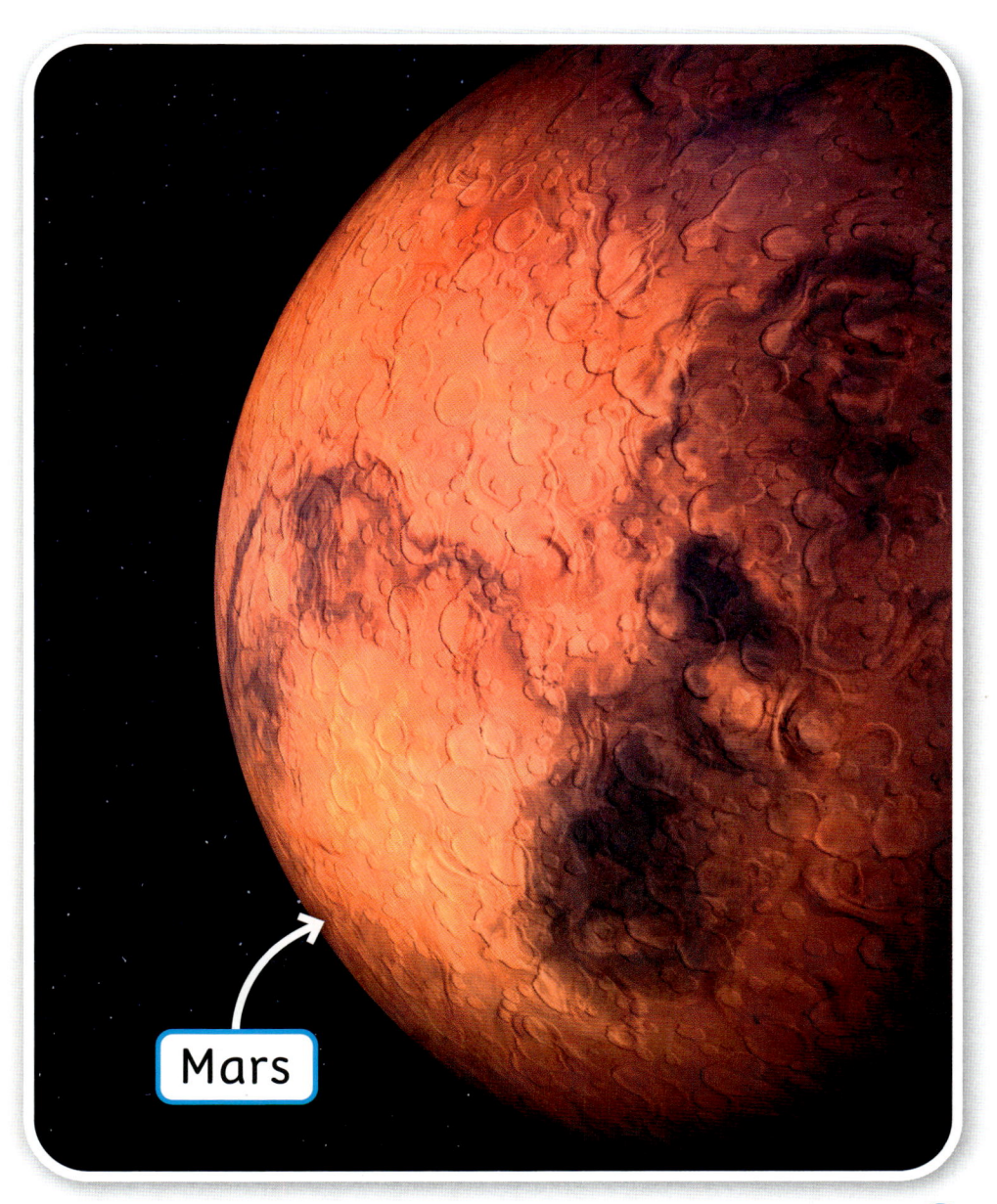

Mars

Can you sort the words on this page into two groups?

Chair

Beard

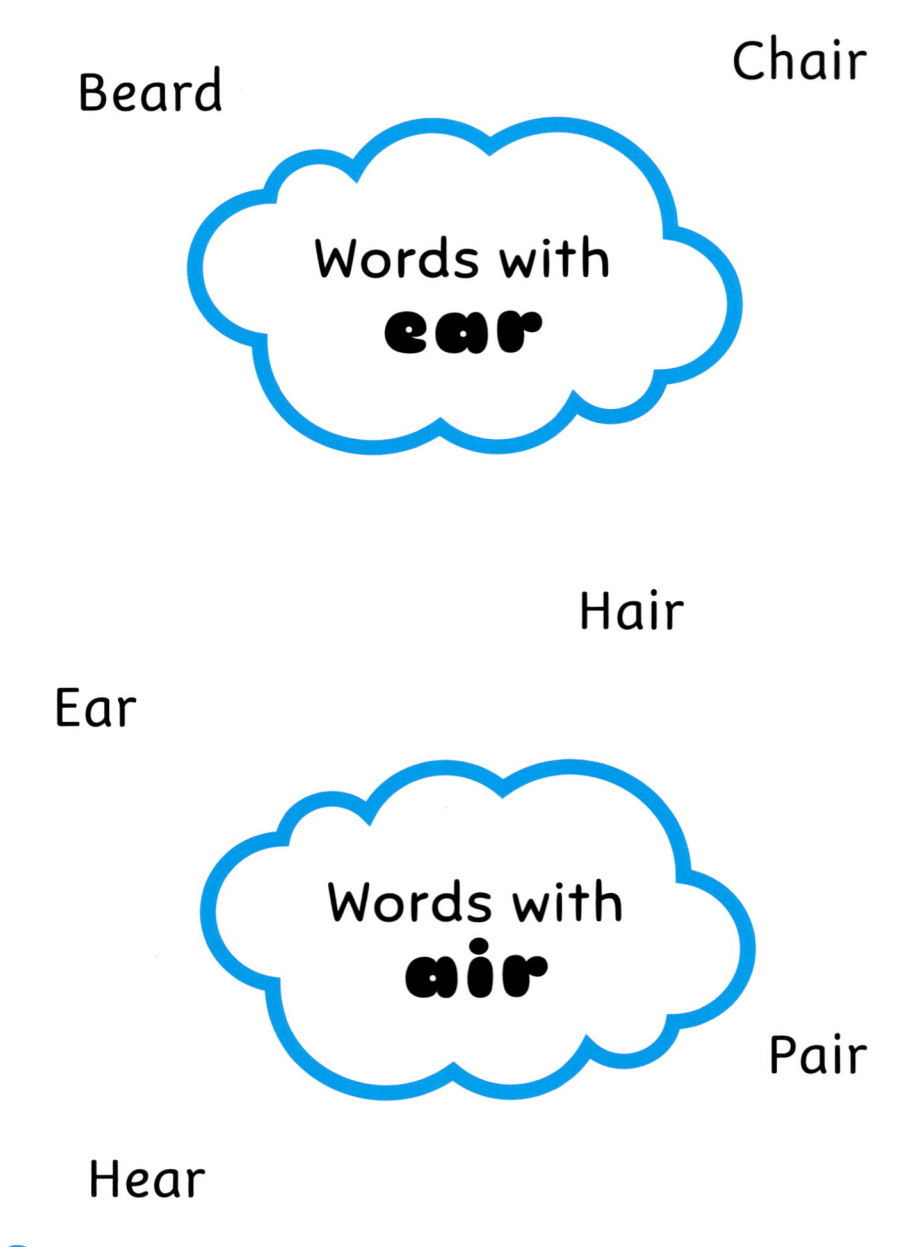

Words with **ear**

Hair

Ear

Words with **air**

Pair

Hear